The Little Book of Goddess Prayers

Immarra Auset

Introduction

Welcome dear reader to my little book of prayers. It is my sincere wish that they assist you in finding a deeper connection to the Goddess in all of her forms. It is important in any spiritual practice to pray. Prayer is a conversation with the divine. Rituals, meditation, worship and spell work are all wonderful things but sometimes we need to just talk to the Divine in order to maintain a deep personal connection.

These prayers can be used when you need them or repeated throughout the day. Some of them could be used as mantras or reflections for meditation. Each prayer has its own page so that its message stands alone.

However you see fit to use them may you ever be blessed by the Goddess.

Prayers to Maiden

The Maiden Goddess is represented by the waxing moon. In myth, She is represented by the young woman wild and free.

O Goddess of the Silver Bow remind me that I too shall grow. Moon of the Maiden Fair, Challenge me to know, to will to dare. Renewal is the blessing of the new moon, reminding us that all shall come but not too soon. O Virgin of the starry sky, grant to me your sacred boon. Grant me renewal with each new moon.

Blessed Maiden,

I give thanks for the laughter in my life and the healing it brings.

I ask that you remind me to laugh long and loud.

Blessed Maiden,

I give you thanks for the constant opportunity to grow.

I ask that you open my eyes to these opportunities and give me the courage to seize them.

Blessed Maiden,

Thank you for your spirit of fearlessness.

I ask that you remind me of the fearless, free spirit within me.

Blessed Maiden,

Help me to forever
carry the blessings of
Spring within my heart.

Let me never forget
the beauty of life
returning after the cold
winter both without
and within.

Blessed Maiden,

Thank you for the Spirit of Adventure.

Let me always seek out the hidden, secret places in life and within myself.

Let me always delight in the finding of them.

Blessed Maiden, Patroness of the Wild Wood,

Guide me in my actions that I may cherish and protect the woodlands as sanctuaries for the soul of all mankind.

Blessed Maiden,
Guardian of Children,

Help me to be kind and patient with the little ones, to see each as a treasure and a joy.

Give me the courage and strength to keep the safe from harm.

Blessed Maiden,

Fair of Form,

Grant to me a youthful spirit that will be beautiful long after youth's first flush is gone.

Blessed Maiden,

May I dance the circle
round with wild
abandon,

For the JOY of it,

All the days of my life.

Blessed Maiden,

May the cleansing rains of Spring fall gently into my life,

Washing away all negativity, illness and strife.

Blessed Maiden,

Remind me to always take time to sit among the flowers of the field.

Let me not only smell them but drink in their beauty feeling their healing energy deep within my soul.

Blessed Maiden,

Give me the boldness to move away from that which is comfortable to the point of stagnation.

Let me seek out growth through movement and exploration.

Blessed Maiden,

Help me to control my fears.

Remind me that when we descend into the Underworld a Maiden, We emerge a Queen.

Blessed Maiden,

Open my ears that I might listen, as a child, to the stories of others and truly hear the lessons within.

Help me to listen that I might be a better friend.

Blessed Maiden,

Engender in me a sense of Wonder.

Let me always be amazed by the beauty of creation all around me.

Blessed Maiden,

Grant me the Joy of Play each and every day.

Blessed Maiden,

Teach me to Sing!

Let me sing deep within my soul.

Let me sing my love, my joy, my pain.

Let me sing until my soul is filled with light again.

Blessed Maiden,

Light within my heart
the sacred flame.

Let me nourish and
tend it.

May it never be
extinguished ever
again.

Blessed Maiden,

Give me the certainty that my Honor is mine alone.

Grant me the courage to define and protect it steadfastly on my own.

Blessed Maiden,

I welcome you into my heart, my hearth and my home.

I know that with your love, I never travel alone.

Blessed Maiden,

Archer of the Waxing Moons Bow,

Let my aim always be true,

Let my words and actions help many and harm few.

Blessed Maiden,

May I always beat the drum and tread the circle round in places where magick is to be found.

Blessed Maiden,
Young and Fair,

May I always live my
life with my own style
and flair!

Blessed Maiden,

In Justice may my arrows fly swift and true.

May they always be fair with each receiving his just due.

Blessed Maiden,

By the light of the
waxing moons glow,

Let me seek upon the
sacred lake the
reflection of my soul.

Reveal unto me the
truth of myself you
would have me know.

Blessed Maiden,

Like the dryads of old, Let me commune with the trees so their wisdom I might know.

Let me learn to dance with the wind,

Be strongly rooted,

Never to break but only to bend.

Blessed Maiden,

I give you thanks for the innocence within me which can never be truly lost only hidden.

Help me to rediscover it each and every day.

Blessed Maiden,

Let me rest with the peace of a tired child,

Deeply and untroubled.

Let me dream sweetly upon gossamer fairy wings.

Blessed Maiden,

I give thanks for all the blessing you bestow. I give thanks for the renewal of the young, brave wild and free spirit within me.

Prayers to the Mother

The full moon represents the Mother Goddess. She is the Universal Mother. She creates, teaches, nourishes and protects all of creation as her children.

Beloved Mother,

Help me to see the sacred spark of Divinity within me.

Help me to cherish and nurture this spark that it may become a great flame against the darkness.

Beloved Mother,

Be a shield unto me this day against those who would drain from me my energy, joy and love.

Let me move through this world in Peace and Happiness this day.

Beloved Mother,

Guide my thoughts and actions this day that I may be a blessings unto others and in doing so inspire others to be a blessing as well.

Beloved Mother,

Open my eyes to the beauty of the world all around me.

I give thanks to you for the perfection of creation and accept it as a gift to be treasured.

Beloved Mother,

**Open my mind to
inspirational thought.**

**Let me see the worth
and potential within
myself realizing all
that I can do.**

Beloved mother,

Give me the Strength
to accept life's
challenges with Grace
and Faith.

Let me learn the
lessons of these
challenges knowing
that they shall pass
and I will be stronger
and wiser for having
faced them.

Beloved Mother,

**Bless me that I may
see that I am enough,**

**Created just as I was
meant to be.**

**Bless me with
acceptance of Self.**

Beloved Mother,

Remove from my heart hate and fear.

Open my eyes, my mind and my heart to the One-ness that connects us all in your light.

Beloved Mother,

I give thanks for your compassion.

Teach me to forgive myself for my shortcomings and mistakes. Help me to release the past in order to create a beautiful tomorrow.

Beloved Mother,

I give thanks that I was created perfectly.

I give thanks that I am perfectly created each day.

Beloved Mother,

I give thanks for the fertile fields of my mind and my soul.

Help me to plant positive, loving seeds and nurture them as they grow.

Beloved Mother,

Be forever welcome in my heart and in my home.

I know that in the grace of your loving presence I can never be alone.

Beloved Mother,

May you protect each
of us as we go about
our day.

Return us to one
another in a safe and
peaceful way.

Beloved Mother,

I give thanks for the abundance of your provision.

May you grant me the ability to provide for my family.

May we never hunger.

Beloved Mother,

Bless my hearth and my home with love, comfort, peace and compassion. Let my home ever be a sanctuary.

Beloved Mother,

Teach me the lessons of Summer.

Let me be creative, productive and fruitful even as the fields of the earth are.

Beloved Mother,

She who controls the tides,

Help me in lifes waves not to struggle but upon them ride for all things good and bad come in their own time.

Beloved Mother,

Thank you for the power to heal another heart with a kind word.

Let me never forget this healing power I wield.

Beloved Mother

By the light of the full moon let me be recharged.

May I ever remember that all I seek is not without but contained within.

Beloved Mother,

I give thanks for the gift of my birth.

Thank you for this opportunity to walk the earth.

Beloved Mother,

I ask that you hold me safe within your loving arms allowing me to feel loved and safe from harm.

Beloved Mother,

Guide me to walk the spiral path in order to find my center deep within.

Teach me the mystery of the spiral that the soul has no beginning and no end.

Beloved Mother,

I give thanks for the fertile green growing earth. Help me to grow into my true purpose and blossom upon recognizing its worth.

Beloved Mother,

I give you thanks for the mysteries of the chalice and the well. Teach me that to be receptive is to journey deep within where a woman's wisdom does dwell.

Beloved Mother,

Bless me with Passion,
Love and Warmth all
the days of my life.

Beloved Mother,

**Let me reflect the
beauty of your love
both day and night,
Even as the full moon
does reflect the suns
light.**

Beloved Mother,

Help me to have to
Strength and Wisdom
to lead with love and
compassion for both
myself and others.

Beloved Mother,

Help me to tend the Garden of my Life that I might harvest the abundance of your blessings without waste and without strife.

Prayers to the Crone

The Crone Goddess is represented by the waning moon. She is depicted as an elderly woman full of wisdom. It is she who controls death and rebirth.

Most Honored Crone,

You are forever welcome in my heart and in my home. For in your presence I am never alone.

Most Honored Crone,

Let me ever remember the lesson of the besom broom:

First you must sweep away negativity before love and light can fill a room.

Most Honored Crone,

Lady of the Sickle
Moon,

Help me to reflect and
with wisdom choose
those things which
from my life need to be
removed.

Most Honored Crone,

Guide me in the lesson
that is winters own,

Teach me to be still
and rest,

To look within and
with wisdom be
blessed.

Most Honored Crone,

I give thanks for your gifts both of death and rebirth with which we have been blessed.

Most Honoured Crone,

Help me to learn the lessons of this lifetime truly and well that I might release them and move on to the next lesson of the chalice well.

Most Honored Crone,

Grant me the understanding that sometimes the only company I need seek is my own.

Most Honored Crone,

Help me to remember all of those who came before me so that I might be who I am today.

I remember my ancestors to you, Oh Goddess.

Most Honored Crone,

Open my mind to the wisdom all around me. Let me seek it out in book, in nature and in the stories of the elders of the world.

Most Honored Crone,

Open my eyes that I might see through the veil of illusion.

Let me see Truth and Reality all around me.

Most Honored Crone,

**Teach me the lesson
of the sickle blade:**

**Only by cutting away
the deadwood can
room for new growth
be made.**

Most Honored Crone,

Grant me the blessing of the deep dark earth.

Grant me strength and solidity.

Most Honored Crone,

Bless me with the wisdom of the cauldron:

Power and vision with great patience and care must be nurtured and tended in order to grow.

Most Honored Crone,

Bless me with the wisdom and strength to protect the peace and sanctity of my hearth and my home.

Most Honored Crone,

Grant me the ability to laugh at myself both when alone or in a crowd.

Most Honored Crone,

Grant me the gift that comes with age.

Let me know myself and heed not what others might say.

Most Honored Crone,

Remind me in hard
times that only in
contrast to the
darkness can the light
be known.

Most Honored Crone,

Teach me this lesson of nature:

To lay aside a portion in times of Harvest to sustain me through the long cold winter.

Most Honored Crone

Grant me a respect for tradition but let me not be a slave to it.

Living tradition links generations.

Most Honored Crone,

Bless me with loyal
and trustworthy
friends.

Bless me with the love
and support of wise
women.

Most Honored Crone,

Bless me with Honor. Let me move through the world in an honourable way and from my own truth and path never sway.

Most Honored Crone,

Teach me to fear not
death for you will be
there to lead me
through the gate
where those who have
gone before await.

Most Honored Crone,

Teach me the art of divination that I might see clearly both the pitfalls and the best path that might await me.

Most Honored Crone,

Bless me with the understanding that magic resides not within the ritual or the tool but within our souls deep and quiet pools.

Most Honored Crone,

I give you thanks for the wise elders of my community.

I will strive to learn from them the accumulated wisdom of their lives.

Most Honored Crone,

I give thanks for all that I am, all that I have and all that I will be.

I will strive to aid those in need.

Most Honored Crone,

I give thanks for the freedom of age.

I give thanks for freedom from vanity,

Freedom from attachment to material things.

I give thanks for the peace age does bring.

Most Honored Crone,

Let no regret in my
heart ever burn,

Only the wisdom of
lessons learned.

Most Honored Crone,

Bless me with the ability to see not only in black and white but in shades of grey for there is never only one right way.

Most Honored Crone,

Let me not place value on emotions that quickly come and go in a flash.

Instead let me treasure those that like the earth abide and last.

Morning Prayer

Blessed be this day newly born.

Blessed be the elements from which it was formed.

Blessed be the Lord and Lady intertwined, who together are the One Divine.

Children's Bedtime Prayer

Lady of the Moon,

Lord of Light,

Keep me safe all through the night.

Message from the Author

I sincerely hope you enjoyed this little volume. May you ever be blessed with the love of the Goddess.

Please leave a review as this is the mainstay of self published authors.

Brightest Blessings,

Immarra Auset

Made in the USA
Middletown, DE
14 May 2020